THE SUMMONING OF EVERYMAN

A MODERN VERSION OF THE MEDIAEVAL MORALITY PLAY

By

HERBERT W...

SAMUEL   FRENCH

LONDON

NEW YORK   TORONTO   SYDNEY   HOLLYWOOD

PREFACE

This version of EVERYMAN was made for Bristol W.E.A.
Players, and produced by them at the 1947 British Drama League
Community Theatre Festival: with it they won the Western Area
Boughton Chatwin Memorial Trophy, and were placed second in
the National Final at the Scala Theatre, subsequently broadcasting
the play on the West of England Home Service.

To tamper with a work of art is generally indefensible. In
the case of EVERYMAN, however, the mediaeval idiom, though
hallowed by tradition, was felt to be an obstacle to general appre-
ciation; even with the pageantry of costume, it might create an
elegant illusion of unreality, reducing the impact of the drama.

That all is vanity, that we can take nothing but our
characters with us when we die, is the theme of EVERYMAN, and
is not for an age but for all time. Perhaps it is not too presumptuous
to hope that performances in present-day speech and costume will
serve as an introduction to the glories of the original.

For the advice and interest of his colleagues, Mr. H. C. Fay,
M.A., and Mr. J. F. Strachan. B.Sc.; for the devotion and tireless
enthusiasm of his friends, the Bristol W.E.A. Players; and for kind-
nesses received in many quarters, the writer is glad to be able to
record his thanks.

TO MY MOTHER

THE SUMMONING OF EVERYMAN

Presented by Bristol W.E.A. Players, on Monday, June 2nd, 1947, at the Scala Theatre, London, on the occasion of the National Final of the British Drama League Community Theatre Festival, with the following cast of characters:—

MESSENGER	Cecil Hodges
THE VOICE OF GOD	
DEATH	George O'Reilly
EVERYMAN	Roger Gilmour
FELLOWSHIP	David Skinner
KINDRED	Harold Stubbs
COUSIN	Hilary Coleman
MAID	Eileen Hope
GOODS	Arnold Tottle
GOOD-DEEDS	Edith Manvell
KNOWLEDGE	Barbara Bees
CONFESSION	Herbert Payne
DISCRETION	Kathleen Brakenridge
STRENGTH	Ian Packer
FIVE-WITS	Joan Vine
BEAUTY	Diana May
ANGEL	Hilary Tottle

Production and Setting : Herbert W. Payne

Producer's Assistant : Marjorie Davey

Lighting : John Strachan

Wardrobe : Marjorie Davey and Barbara Bees

Stage Direction and Scene Construction : George O'Reilly

THE SUMMONING OF EVERYMAN

A MODERN VERSION OF THE MEDIAEVAL MORALITY

The scene is in two levels. Upstage R., *prominent against a plain background, there is a great cross. A high platform,* C., *divides the upper level into unequal parts :* L. *of the platform a depression to the lower stage level symbolises* EVERYMAN'S *grave : to the* L. *again, golden steps rise into the wings. If the background is a cyclorama it should be lit with deep blue.*

The upstage level is framed by narrow curtains and descends to the lower plane by means of a long, shallow step R.C.

DEATH *stands on the high platform, looking towards steps, and* GOOD-DEEDS *is lying at the foot of the grave.*

When the Curtain rises the stage is in darkness : a shaft of light is directed on the entrance down R.

Enter a MESSENGER, *as Prologue.*

MESSENGER. Ladies and Gentlemen, *The Summoning of Everyman,* a moral play. Our story says, "Man, when you are young, think well, remember your ending. You are strong, healthy, successful : you enjoy life : never forget that one day you must die. Sin seems very attractive at first : it will bring tears and sorrow to your soul when your body lies in clay." In this morality the King of Heaven calls Everyman to his last account. Listen then, and hear God speak.

(Exit MESSENGER. *A light appears on the steps.* GOD *speaks.)*

GOD. From My high throne in Heaven I see all men living without dread, thinking only on worldly prosperity: drowned in sin, they forget that I am God. They forget my law that I showed them when I died, and they forget My red blood that I shed for their redemption. I showed the people great mercy, but few there be that ask it eagerly. Therefore I will call Everyman to a reckoning. For if I leave the people alone they will become much worse than beasts, having no charity in their hearts. Where art thou, Death, thou mighty messenger?

(The light fades in on the platform. DEATH *speaks.)*

7

DEATH. Almighty God, I am here to do Thy will.

GOD. Go thou to Everyman, and show him, in My name, a pilgrimage he must undertake, which he cannot escape, and that he must bring his life's reckoning with him, and come without delay.

(The light on the steps slowly fades.)

DEATH. Lord, I will go about the world. I will seek out small and great who neglect Thy law. Everyman will I strike. Unless he repent, his soul shall live in Hell. There is Everyman walking. He little expects my coming. He is thinking of lust and riches.

(Enter EVERYMAN *from the auditorium.)*

Everyman, stand still. Where are you going in your fine clothes? Have you forgotten your Maker?

EVERYMAN. Why do you ask that?

DEATH. Almighty God has sent me.

EVERYMAN. What, to me?

DEATH. Yes. God remembers you.

EVERYMAN. What does God want with me?

DEATH. A reckoning

EVERYMAN. A reckoning! *(He laughs.)* I shall need time for that!

DEATH. God calls you to go on a long journey; and bring your reckoning with you, for you will not be able to return: and let it be a true one, so that you may answer for all your many bad deeds, and your few good ones, before the Lord Himself.

EVERYMAN. But I'm not ready! Besides, who are you, bringing a message like that?

DEATH. I am Death!

EVERYMAN. Death! I'd forgotten you. Well, of course, Death, you can save me. I'll give you a thousand pounds if you'll wait till another day!

DEATH. I set no store by gold, nor kings, nor any power on earth Come! Your journey! No more delay!

EVERYMAN. But .. surely I can take my friends with me?

DEATH. Yes, if they are brave enough!

EVERYMAN. The grave and all my sins! What a fool! What a fool! How can I get away? Oh, Death, good Death let me off till to-morrow, so that I can repent of my sins!

DEATH. None will I respite. Death is sudden. Death strikes without warning, to the very heart. Therefore, make ready, for this is the day that no man living may escape.

(Exit DEATH *up the steps. The light fades.)*

EVERYMAN. Ah, no Death, no! Ah, Death! God, I've got something to cry about now! Nobody here! Nobody to help me! I shall die, and no-one to go with me! And my reckoning! I haven't made my reckoning! Oh, I wish to God I'd never been born! Time's flying! I must do something. Lord God, Maker of all things, help me now! God help me! . . . No good! The day's passing, the day's passing, it's nearly gone. There must be someone. Who can I get . . who . . . who?

(The spot down L. fades in.)

Fellowship! Yes, Fellowship! Just the man! We've always been together. There he is! Fellowship! He's bound to come, of course he will.

(Enter FELLOWSHIP down L.)

Oh, Fellowship!

FELLOWSHIP. Everyman, how are you? Hullo, you look worried!

EVERYMAN. Oh, Fellowship, for the Lord's sake help me. I'm in mortal danger!

(No. 1 Batten fades in ¼.)

FELLOWSHIP. Mortal danger? My dear chap. Tell me all about it. Of course I'll help.

EVERYMAN. Oh, thanks, a thousand times.

FELLOWSHIP. Rubbish, man! Two straws for your thanks! But I hate to see you panic. Are you really in a fix?

EVERYMAN. Yes . . .

FELLOWSHIP. Life-long enemy doing his worst. And you're out for a spot of revenge, so to speak? Very right and proper! You can rely on me! It's nothing, nothing at all. I'll do all I possibly can! To the death, my boy! With both eyes open!

EVERYMAN. I knew I could depend on you Fellowship.

FELLOWSHIP. We'll go to Hell together!

EVERYMAN. You're a real friend!

FELLOWSHIP. Spare my blushes! And now, what's the trouble?

EVERYMAN. Well, someone has brought me a message. I've got to go on a journey . . . a long, dangerous journey . . .

FELLOWSHIP. Where?

EVERYMAN. To God.

FELLOWSHIP. God?

EVERYMAN. To tell Him all about myself . . . everything I've ever done.

FELLOWSHIP. That's a bit . . . grim . . . isn't it?

EVERYMAN. Fellowship, I'm scared! Come with me! You must! You promised.

FELLOWSHIP. Certainly, I did . . . and promise is duty! Of course . . . there are duties and duties, if you take my meaning. Now if I went on this trip, I can see it would upset all my arrangements . . besides . . . it's rather fierce, you know!

EVERYMAN. But you said . . .

FELLOWSHIP. I agree, absolutely! All the same . . . when should we get back?

EVERYMAN. Never . . . till Doomsday.

FELLOWSHIP. Doomsday? Who told you all this?

EVERYMAN. He was here just now.

FELLOWSHIP. Who was?

EVERYMAN. Death!

FELLOWSHIP. Death? . . . Death! . . . .Oh. I'm terribly sorry! I couldn't travel on that line! Not for any man!

EVERYMAN. Fellowship, we've been friends for God knows how long! Don't . . . don't desert me!

FELLOWSHIP. Friendship or no friendship, I won't have anything to do with it! Don't keep on at me! Drink, women, robbery . . . murder . . . I'd come, like a shot . . . but Death! Oh, no, that's a poisonous business. I won't have any dealings with Death.

EVERYMAN. You're not walking out on me, now?

FELLOWSHIP. I certainly am! Rely on God, old man . . . not me!

EVERYMAN. Fellowship! . . . I shall never see you again!

FELLOWSHIP. I suppose you won't. Well, good-bye, Everyman . . . Of course I won't forget you. Parting's a grim business and all that, but . . . well . . I . . . I . . well . . Good-bye!

(Exit FELLOWSHIP down L.)

EVERYMAN. Fellowship of all people! Now! Just when I needed him most! What can I do? Who in the world . . friends . . . relations . . . relations! Yes, relations! I'll tell them what a frightful mess I'm in . . . they'll do it, of course they will! Cousin . . . Kindred . . . where are you?

KINDRED *(off)*. That sounds like Everyman . . .

(Enter KINDRED, COUSIN and MAID, down R.)

We heard you calling, Everyman. What do you want?

COUSIN. Are you going off somewhere. dear Cousin? Would you like us to come with you? We will, you know! Anywhere! Come weal, come woe. we'll live and die together!

KINDRED. In any kind of weather! The family, my boy! Always rely on the family!

EVERYMAN. Dear Cousins, thanks, best thanks. Now, listen, I'm in great trouble I've had a message, from somebody most important, a king, a great king. I've got to start at once on a very dangerous

journey, a kind of pilgrimage and . . . I know I shall never come
back. And besides all this, when I get there I've got to render
an account . . a true account . . .

KINDRED. What sort of account?

EVERYMAN. Everything! How I've ever lived, all my sins, all the
decent things I might have done, and haven't; everything, ever
since I was born. I can't go alone, I can't . . . you must come with
me . . . you must . . please! For God's sake come and help me
make up my wretched account?

COUSIN. That sort of journey! Us? You want us . . Oh, I
should think not, indeed! I'd rather live on bread and water for
five years!

EVERYMAN. You can't let me go alone, you can't! Kindred, if
you walk out on me now, I shall go mad, I can't stand it I tell
you . . .

KINDRED. Nonsense, my boy, nonsense! What's come over you?
You've always been a lighthearted chap . . . plenty of guts . . .
game for anything! Where's your optimism? Come along, now,
stop this moaning . . . cheer up. But, mind, I'm not going on that
journey.

EVERYMAN. Cousin, dear Cousin, you'll come won't you?

COUSIN. Oh, I couldn't, really I couldn't. For one thing I get
cramp in my toe when I travel! . . You can have my Maid if
you like. She loves gadding about . . . going out to dinner, and
dancing, and all that sort of thing. She can go and help you . . .
I don't mind at all . . . If you think you'll get on together. You
mustn't dream of relying on me. I should only let you down at
the psychological moment.

EVERYMAN. You're joking. You must be! For God's sake,
Kindred, are you coming or are you staying behind?

KINDRED. I'm afraid I must. Stay behind that is, of course! If
you don't mind! . . . Well . . . you're busy . . we mustn't keep
you. Good-bye, my boy . . . Till we meet again . . . Good-bye!

(*Exit* KINDRED, *down* R.)

EVERYMAN. "Where's your optimism?" . . . *Optimism*! . . . *Oh,
God*!

COUSIN Cousin Everyman . . . Cousin Everyman . . . good-bye!
. . . I can't come, really, you know. Just between ourselves I've some
accounts of my own to do. They're nothing like ready, I do assure
you! So you see, I really must be going. Good-bye, dear Cousin . . .
God bless you . . . Good-bye!

(*Exit* COUSIN *and* MAID, *down* R.)

EVERYMAN. Talk, talk! Talk away! Promise the earth! "In any

kind of weather . . . good-bye, dear Cousin!" . . . Friends, relations,
what's the use of them? Nobody's any use! I might just as well
rely on my Goods! Goods! Why not? I've always been mad on
my Goods! I will! Goods, Goods, Goods! My friend Goods and
Riches, where are you?

(The voice of Goods *is heard, off* L.)

Goods *(off)*. Who's that calling? Is that you, Everyman?
Everyman. Yes, come here, Goods, quickly!
Goods *(off)*. What a hurry you're in! I can hardly get out. Cash-
boxes, furniture, pictures, jewellery. piled up to the ceiling! There
isn't a square inch anywhere . . . And all these bags . . .

(Enter Goods, *down* L.)

. . . There, that's better! What a struggle! Well, what do you
want?
Everyman. I want your advice.
Goods. And for that, sir, I'm your man. All the troubles, all the
hardships in the world, I just charm them away!
Everyman. It isn't the world, Goods. Quite another place! Listen!
I've been sent for . . . by God! I've got to go to Him at once, and
make a clean breast of everything I've ever done. Now, you're just
the man I want! I've always been fond of you, Goods, and I want
you to come with me, and clean my slate a bit for God. You know
the Bible says money answers all things . . . .
Goods. No! . . .No! . . . No expeditions of that kind for me!
Oh, no! I should only make matters worse. Who do you think
smeared your slate, anyway? I did! You've been far too fond
of me, my friend. That's why you can't do your own reckoning.
Now, if you'd ever thought of giving a trifle of me to the poor!
You can't take me with you, you know.
Everyman. I thought I could.
Goods. Yes! And that's why Goods is a thief of souls.
Everyman. You damned hypocrite! A traitor to God, that's what
you are! You've led me on! You've caught me in your trap . . .
Goods. Rubbish! You've nobody to blame but yourself. And a
good thing, too! Upon my word, it's very funny! I can't help
laughing!
Everyman. Listen, Goods! Because I've loved you . . . all my
life . . . more than I've ever loved God himself . . . you must come
. . . you must show me how to make my reckoning . . .
Goods. God help us, no, no, no! And I can't stay here gossiping.
I'm much too busy! So, good-bye to you . . . and good luck!

(Exit Goods, *down* R.)

EVERYMAN. "Goods is a thief of souls!" Oh, God, I feel so ashamed! What can I do? What can I do? There must be something . . . I wonder . . . perhaps I should have some luck with my Good-Deeds. My Good-Deeds! What a hope! She's such a miserable thing . . . anyhow I can but try. Good-Deeds, where are you? Good-Deeds . . .

(GOOD-DEEDS *looks up.*)

GOOD-DEEDS. Here, Everyman. It is cold lying on the ground. Your sins have bound me. I cannot move
EVERYMAN. Oh, Good-Deeds, tell me what to do. I'm so frightened.
GOOD-DEEDS. I know, Everyman God has sent for you.
EVERYMAN. Yes. Go with me, please.
GOOD-DEEDS. I would gladly, but you see I cannot stand . . .
EVERYMAN. Please try. I do need you so. Help me make my reckoning, or I shall be damned for ever.

(*Enter* KNOWLEDGE *down* R.)

GOOD-DEEDS. I'm sorry, Everyman. If I only could . . .
EVERYMAN. Then give me some advice.
GOOD-DEEDS. Yes, I will do that. See, here is my sister. Her name is Knowledge. She will stand by you, and help you with your solemn reckoning.

(*The spot fades in on the Cross.*)

EVERYMAN. Knowledge, of course! Knowledge can save me!
KNOWLEDGE. I will go with you, Everyman, and be your guide.
EVERYMAN. Thanks be to God!
GOOD-DEEDS. And when you have repented, and your sins are forgiven, you must take your account, and your Good-Deeds, and start on your journey. And when you come before the Blessed Trinity . . .
EVERYMAN. Then . . .

(*Enter* CONFESSION, *up* R.)

GOOD-DEEDS. Your heart will be filled with joy.
EVERYMAN. Oh, Good-Deeds, I don't know how to thank you!
KNOWLEDGE. Let us go now, Everyman, to Confession.
EVERYMAN. Where does he live?
KNOWLEDGE. In the House of Salvation. Come, we shall find him there; he will comfort us by God's Grace.
EVERYMAN. Oh, Glorious Fountain, cleansing all uncleanness, wash me thoroughly from my wickedness: let no spots of sin be seen on me when I go to my last account.

(KNOWLEDGE *leads* EVERYMAN *to the step* R., *above which*
CONFESSION *is standing.*)

KNOWLEDGE. Kneel down, and ask for mercy. He can help you.
God loves him.

(EVERYMAN *kneels on the step, and seizes* CONFESSION'S *arm.*)

EVERYMAN. Confession, please listen, and help my Good-Deeds.
CONFESSION. I know your sorrow, Everyman. I will comfort you
as best I can. I bring you a precious jewel, a scourge, called penance.
Let it remind you how your Saviour was scourged for your sake.
You, too, must scourge yourself. Your body, partner of your sins,
you must mortify with denial and abstinence : direct your heart
and mind to God, and walk in His ways. Strengthen him, Knowledge, see that he makes amends, and when he has done. Good-
Deeds will be here. Courage, Everyman. Say your prayers, and
ask God for mercy. He will not fail you.

(*He blesses* EVERYMAN. *Exit* CONFESSION, *up* R. EVERYMAN *mounts
the upstage level, to the right of the high platform, and stands
where* CONFESSION *had stood.*)

EVERYMAN. God be thanked! Now I am happy again!

(KNOWLEDGE *mounts the upstage level, and stands extreme* R.)

KNOWLEDGE. Do not forget your penance, Everyman.
EVERYMAN. Oh, Blessed God, forgive me all my wickedness; forgive the sins of the flesh! You were too soft, body; you would have
me damned for ever! Take this penance, body, for a scourging and
punishment. Lust no more, and wait upon God.

(EVERYMAN *goes to the Cross and kneels. During the following speech*
GOOD-DEEDS *slowly raises herself, and mounts the upstage level.*)

   " Have mercy upon me, oh God, according to Thy loving
kindness . . . .
   " Purge me . . . and I shall be clean; wash me, and I shall be
whiter than snow.
   " Oh, Lord, open Thou my lips: and my mouth shall show
forth Thy praise.
   " For Thou desirest not sacrifice, else would I give it: thou
delightest not in burnt offering.
   " The sacrifices of God are a broken spirit: a broken and a
contrite heart, oh God, thou wilt not despise."
   Oh, water of penance, save me from the fires of Purgatory!

GOOD-DEEDS. Thank God, I can walk, I am well again! Everyman, I will go with you now, and help give an account of your good works.

EVERYMAN. My Good-Deeds! Oh, I am thankful to hear your voice again!

KNOWLEDGE. Forget your sadness, Everyman. Contrition will bring you forgiveness. God loves a contrite heart.

EVERYMAN. Blessed be Jesus, Mary's son, for He has given me the garment of contrition, and made me sorry for my sins. And now, let's go at once. Is my reckoning all right?

GOOD-DEEDS. It is a good reckoning.

EVERYMAN. At last! Dear God, I hope I need not be afraid. You are my friends. You won't leave me, will you?

KNOWLEDGE. No, Everyman.

GOOD-DEEDS. There are three others you must take with you. Very important, all of them.

EVERYMAN. Three others? Who?

GOOD-DEEDS. They are your friends, too. Discretion, Strength and Beauty.

KNOWLEDGE. And Five-Wits to give you good advice.

EVERYMAN. Of course! My friends, where are you? Discretion, Strength! Come here, quickly! Five-Wits. Beauty!

(*Enter* BEAUTY, *down* R., FIVE-WITS, STRENGTH *and* DISCRETION, *down* L.)

BEAUTY. We heard you calling, Everyman; here we are you see. What do you want us for?

GOOD-DEEDS. Everyman is going on a pilgrimage to present his true account. He is in great need. You are his friends. Will you go with him?

STRENGTH. To the very end: and help him, as much as we possibly can. You can trust me.

DISCRETION. Discretion, too. We shall all go. Of course!

EVERYMAN. Almighty God, I praise Thee for my Strength . . .

STRENGTH. I will stand by you, Everyman: in any kind of trouble.

EVERYMAN. My Five-Wits . . .

FIVE-WITS. All the world over, I will never leave you.

EVERYMAN. My Beauty . . .

BEAUTY. Nor I, Everyman, till my dying day.

EVERYMAN. Discretion . . .

DISCRETION. You must plan things first, and move cautiously of course. but you may rest assured that all will be well.

EVERYMAN. Good-Deeds and Knowledge, too! All I need to help me. God bless you! Now, listen, everyone. I'll make my will: half my goods to charity, the other half back where it belongs . . .

KNOWLEDGE. And now, Everyman, I advise you to go and see

your priest. Receive the Sacrament, be anointed with holy oil. Then come here again: we will all wait for you.

FIVE-WITS. Hurry, or you may be too late.

EVERYMAN. Yes, yes. I want to receive the Blesséd Sacrament. I'll go at once.

(*Exit* EVERYMAN, *up* R.)

FIVE-WITS. That's best for Everyman! Why do we put our trust in princes, when we might have the Grace of God? The Holy Sacraments, I mean, to strengthen and redeem our souls. It's a wonderful thing to be the minister of God's Grace: His power and glory. Dictators have their day, and parliaments and plans· they don't amount to much when Everyman is waiting to die. Only God's Sacrifice can help him then, and God's ambassador, the holy priest.

KNOWLEDGE. The holy priest is God's ambassador: and so is Everyman when he repents.

FIVE-WITS. "All we, like sheep, have gone astray." God send us good shepherds, and guide us safely home. Quiet! There's Everyman coming. He's all right now.

GOOD-DEEDS. Yes, it is Everyman.

(*Enter* EVERYMAN, *up* R.)

EVERYMAN. Lord God I thank Thee for giving me Thyself in this Blesséd Sacrament, for the gift of my extreme unction. My good friends, bless you all for waiting so long. (*He shows a crucifix.*) Look! here is my crucifix. Come and put your hands upon it.

(*They all do so,* KNOWLEDGE *and* GOOD-DEEDS *first, standing on the upper level with* EVERYMAN; *then the others, on the lower level, move in to touch the crucifix,* BEAUTY *in the centre of the group and kneeling on the step.* KNOWLEDGE *and* GOOD-DEEDS *return to their former positions on the upper level;* STRENGTH, DISCRETION *and* FIVE-WITS *take up new positions on the lower level;* BEAUTY *remains kneeling. The light fades in on the platform.*)

And now let us go. Come! I lead the way. I know the place where I long to be. God guide us!

(EVERYMAN *now mounts the high platform.*)

STRENGTH. Count on me, Everyman! To the end!

DISCRETION. I shall be with you, Everyman.

KNOWLEDGE. I shall never leave you, however hard your pilgrimage may be.

EVERYMAN. I'm so faint. I can't stand: my limbs are giving

way . . . No going back: we mustn't go back; not for all the money in the world.

(EVERYMAN *looks into his grave.* BEAUTY, *who has mounted to the upper level, is standing by the side of the high platform.*)

Here is the cave I must creep into . . . and turn to the earth. . . . and sleep.

BEAUTY. What, into this grave? Oh!

EVERYMAN. Yes, this grave, where we shall crumble and rot, all alike.

BEAUTY. What! Shall I smother here, too?

EVERYMAN. Yes . . . and never be seen again. We shall never live in this world again; only in Heaven with Almighty God.

(BEAUTY *descends to the lower level* R.)

BEAUTY. I can't do it! Sorry, dear Everyman, you must count me out! I'll kiss my hand, and leave you.

EVERYMAN. Beauty, where are you going?

BEAUTY. It's no use! I can't hear! I wouldn't stay, if you offered me all the money in your bank!

(*Exit* BEAUTY, *down* R. *The spot down* R. *fades to* $\frac{1}{2}$.)

EVERYMAN. O God, you gave me my gifts. Don't take them away! Now, Beauty's going, and she promised to live and die with me.

STRENGTH. I'll be leaving you now, Everyman, as well. I don't like this game at all.

EVERYMAN. You're all deserting me! Oh, Strength, Strength, stay just a little while.

STRENGTH. Not for the world. Not if you cry your heart out. I'm moving, just as fast as my legs can carry me.

EVERYMAN. But you promised! You won't break your promise?

STRENGTH. Never mind my promises. I've come far enough, and you're old enough to look after yourself. What a fool you are, wasting your energy, whining and complaining. Get into the ground!

(*Exit* STRENGTH, *down* L. *The spot down* L. *fades to* $\frac{1}{2}$.)

EVERYMAN. I thought I should keep my Strength . . . they've both cheated me.

DISCRETION. Well, now Strength has departed, I must follow his example. As far as I'm concerned you'll have to go alone.

EVERYMAN. Discretion, you as well?

DISCRETION. Yes, I'm afraid that is the position. When Strength leads the way I always follow.

EVERYMAN. For God's sake be a little sorry for me! Look once in my grave.

DISCRETION. No, I'll not come so near as that. Farewell everyone.

(*Exit* DISCRETION, *down* L. *The spot down* R. *fades out.*)

EVERYMAN. All things fail, except God. Beauty, Strength, Discretion, they're leaving me as fast as they can.

FIVE-WITS. I'll say good-bye now, Everyman.

EVERYMAN. Five-Wits! I took you for my best friend!

FIVE-WITS. I've no more time for you Good-bye and that's that!

(*Exit* FIVE-WITS, *down* L. *The spot down* L. *fades out.*)

EVERYMAN. Oh, Lord Jesus, help! They've all deserted me!

GOOD-DEEDS. No, Everyman. You shall find me with you at the last.

EVERYMAN. Oh, Good-Deeds, I'm so thankful you're still here! Now I can see who my true friends are. And to think I once loved them more than you! Knowledge, will you desert me too?

KNOWLEDGE. When you die I shall, Everyman. Not yet, for any danger.

EVERYMAN. It's almost time. I think I must make my reckoning, and go to pay my debts.

(EVERYMAN *looks to the audience. No.* 1 *Batten fades out.*)

Take warning, you who hear and see me now. Everything I loved best in the world is gone: everyone has deserted me, except my Good-Deeds, my best of friends.

GOOD-DEEDS. All earthly things are vanity. Beauty, Strength, Discretion · foolish friends, plausible relations: all forsake a man at the last: all save Good-Deeds, and that am I.

EVERYMAN. Have mercy on me, Most Mighty God: stand by me Mary, Holy Maid and Mother!

(GOOD-DEEDS *mounts the high platform, behind* EVERYMAN.)

GOOD-DEEDS. Fear not, Everyman. I will speak for you.

(*The light on the Cross fades out.*)

EVERYMAN. Into Thy hands, Lord, I commend my spirit. Take it, Lord! Don't let it be lost! As Thou boughtest me, so defend me. Save me from Satan! Let me appear with all the blessed host that shall be saved at the day of doom. *In manus tuas . . .!* for ever . . . *commendo spiritum meum!*

Black-out.

(*During the last sentence,* EVERYMAN *sinks into his grave, followed by* GOOD-DEEDS. *There is darkness all over the stage.*)

KNOWLEDGE. Now, he has suffered death, just as we all shall die. Good-Deeds shall make his peace with God. He has finished his course on earth: angels in heaven, rejoice, and sing for Everyman, returning home.

(*While* KNOWLEDGE *is speaking a light gradually suffuses the golden steps, and an angel is seen standing there. The angel raises* EVERYMAN *from his grave. The blue light fades in on the cyclorama.*)

ANGEL. Come, splendid bride of Jesus; thy reckoning is crystal clear. Now shalt thou see thy Father's face, and dwell with Him for ever: to Whose eternal mansions, all ye that love the Lord, and walk in His ways, shall come, like Everyman, at last.

(*The* ANGEL *leads away* EVERYMAN *and* GOOD-DEEDS. KNOWLEDGE *waits until they have departed, and then goes out, up* R. *The light on the golden steps fades, and the entrance light down* R. *comes on. The* MESSENGER *is disclosed there, for the Epilogue.*)

MESSENGER. That is our moral. Give up Pride: he cheats you in the end. Beauty, Strength, Discretion, Five-Wits, all forsake a man at the last. Only Good-Deeds goes with him there, and if she is small, nothing, no excuses, can help him before God. What can he do then? If his reckoning is not clear at his coming God will say, "Go, ye wicked, into everlasting fire." But he who presents his true account shall be crowned high in Heaven. God bring us all there, to live body and soul together! May the Trinity help us to do it! Please say "Amen", for Holy Charity.

So ends this moral play of EVERYMAN.

PRODUCTION NOTES

The following notes refer to the original production. They should be regarded as informatory and suggestive, not as imposing an invariable design. For this reason stage directions in the text have been reduced to a minimum. Imaginative producers will find the story a sufficient stimulus.

This modern version is not, of course, a "stunt". A chromium-plated cocktail bar, with DR. DEATH giving the dissipated EVERYMAN three months to live might be an arresting first scene, but would probably turn out to belong to a different play.

Consistency and dignity will be ensured if the story is treated as a psychological drama. EVERYMAN realises the approach of Death. In his first fear he turns to friends, relations, even possessions: they fail him, and from that moment he is really alone. All the subsequent characters, with the possible exception of CONFESSION, are merely projections of his imagination. He never touches them, and even turning in their direction looks beyond, seeing them only in his mind's eye.

The production should be simple, natural and restrained. Any artificialities of speech, gesture or movement would be out of place.

Setting

A photograph and plan of the setting as used for the first production are included. The stage directions refer to this setting, but producers who wish to experiment will, no doubt, evolve vital and dignified conceptions of their own.

Ground-Plan

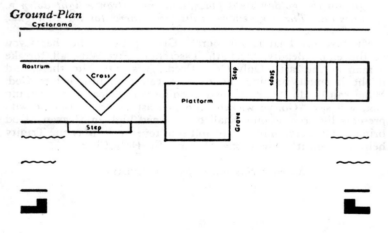

Lighting
Floods and spots give the most suitable effect: three up-stage, for the steps, centre rostrum and cross, and two down-stage, one R. and one L., are sufficient. It may be necessary to use a very little No. 1 Batten to light down-stage c. during the middle of the play. Otherwise the effect to aim at is pools of light in surrounding shadow. If a cyclorama is available, deep midnight blue makes a beautiful background. The other mediums should be white, amber and pink.

Costume and Make-Up
There is more scope for originality in modern dress than might at first be thought, but perhaps it should be remembered that EVERYMAN is any man, so that the fantastic or unusual is unsuitable either for him or for any of the human characters.

EVERYMAN, neither very young nor very old, is probably well-to-do —he is fond of his GOODS—a man about town. He should be well dressed, and his make-up should indicate the worldly and slightly dissolute.

FELLOWSHIP should be a younger, more careless and more robust likeness of EVERYMAN.

KINDRED in this version has been conceived as a man, COUSIN as a woman. They should be over-fashionably arrayed, exuding health and prosperity. Their MAID must correspond.

CONFESSION is a priest: he should wear a cassock, cotta or surplice, and a violet stole. His blessing should be given with three fingers of the right hand.

GOODS, who may be considered a bridge between the human characters and the qualities, might be dressed in "city" garments and furnished with cheque books, brief-cases or any properties suggesting affluence. He may be a rich and jovial type, or a lean and avaricious "Scrooge".

The qualities, BEAUTY, STRENGTH and DISCRETION, lend themselves to varied treatments. Their costumes should be slightly exaggerated "human" fashions: their make-up should also be stylised and intensified, to suggest immateriality. In the original production BEAUTY was a girl, STRENGTH a man, and DISCRETION an older girl. FIVE-WITS is the most difficult: she was portrayed as a sophisticated, but agreeable opportunist, a little too smartly dressed, too well made-up.

KNOWLEDGE and GOOD-DEEDS, both women, present the greatest difficulty. Obvious solutions, such as an outright academic garb for the one, and a nun's or nurse's costume for the other, are not ideal, since they particularize too much: symbolic robes are best, and give scope for ingenuity.

DEATH and the ANGEL demand tact and skill. Bones or funereal weeds would be as regrettable for the first as a tin halo and cotton-wool wings for the second.

A striking DEATH may be created by the use of a black cassock, covering the feet, a long, black "Cowley" cloak, enveloping the body, with the hood down, and a piece of fine, black muslin completely covering the face, head and neck: if the face is painted white to eliminate all shadows, a suitable unearthly effect is obtained.

The ANGEL should be tall, and draped in robes of two colours; silver and mediaeval blue are very effective: the hair, preferably fair, should be unadorned: feet should be bare. The player will be standing in a bright light, so her make-up must be strong, discreet and flawless.

MADE AND PRINTED IN GREAT BRITAIN BY
LATIMER TREND & COMPANY LTD PLYMOUTH
MADE IN ENGLAND